Leadership

An Authoritative Guide Featuring An Exploration Of Primal Leadership And Self-deception, Along With Practical Advice And Strategies For Enhancing Communication Proficiency And Influencing The Psychological Dynamics Of Persuasion

Robert Osborne

TABLE OF CONTENT

Criminal PsychologyAnd Corporate Analogy 1

Exhibiting Leadership Qualities in Thought and Action 5

Managing Change Effectively 22

The Honest Leader 37

Exude positivity and provide heartfelt motivation 42

Leadership Attributes Pertaining to Decision-Making and Crisis Management 56

Acquaint yourself with the Significance of Non-Verbal Communication 89

Physical activity proves to be the most efficacious approach for coping with a difficult day. 119

Criminal Psychology And Corporate Analogy

The field of criminal psychology analytics offers insights into prospective criminal behaviors that individuals may exhibit as adults by carefully examining and analyzing the behavior of children in accordance with societal norms of acceptability. As a result, this study has the potential to mitigate instances of emotional outbursts culminating in criminal behavior during the child's transition into adolescence or adulthood. The apprehension, subsequent to the examination, lies in the notion that continual monitoring of the psychological elements in undisciplined juveniles right from the onset could facilitate the implementation of appropriate corrective measures. Subsequently, initiating proper treatment endeavors may aid in curtailing the potential adverse future behaviors (such as violent emotional outbursts leading to criminal conduct) exhibited by these unruly individuals when they reach adulthood. By doing so, we could potentially mitigate instances of future violence within our society and contribute to fostering a tranquil environment for the younger generation. It is advisable to carry out analogous analytical inquiries on employees at regular intervals, such as yearly or half-yearly, regarding their execution of corporate tasks, level of professional appreciation, comprehensive evaluations, engagement in organizational activities, and so forth. This will allow for the anticipation of employees' professional qualities in terms of compliance with corporate protocols and relationships, thereby mitigating any potential negative occurrences within the corporate sphere.

Psychological perspective: Psychology is an intricately complex field of Science that unveils the behavioral patterns of individuals. Research in the field of child psychology has indicated that it is possible, albeit with some margin of error, to anticipate the future propensity for violent behavior in individuals who exhibited violent tendencies during their childhood, which may manifest in adulthood. For instance, in the case where a child has experienced abuse, it is probable that a sense of animosity has formed within them, manifesting as a tendency towards emotional outbursts when provoked. This psychological aspect has been convincingly supported through analytical examination of 'criminal confessions' obtained during interrogations. In a similar vein, it is necessary to record and organize the professional qualities of an employee within a specified timeframe, encompassing both inter-departmental and intra-departmental relationships within the organization. This process is essential for determining and establishing effective team-building strategies, providing guidance and support, fostering a positive work environment, and considering opportunities for advancement. Consequently, over time, the organization would experience an elevation in the magnitude of its profitability.

LESSON ON CORPORATE BEHAVIOR: By examining the behavioral patterns of employees within and across different departments of a corporation, as well as their work patterns focused on achieving outcomes, in the context of a disciplined corporate culture, one can objectively identify and analyze factors that can forecast the impact of employee involvement on corporate profitability. This, in turn, facilitates informed decision-making and minimizes the occurrence of undesirable outcomes in the future operations of the corporation.

Exhibiting Leadership Qualities in Thought and Action

Prior to attaining the status of an authentic leader, it is imperative to engage in cognitive and behavioral patterns akin to those exhibited by successful leaders. This chapter will provide instruction on cultivating the mentality and behavior of a leader, with the aim of facilitating your transformation into a leader over time. These are uncomplicated procedures that may necessitate a certain amount of time and exertion, but will ultimately be of great value.

Be people-oriented

Effective leadership necessitates the establishment of strong interpersonal connections with individuals. Given your role as their guide, it is crucial to possess a thorough understanding of their character and to demonstrate genuine empathy towards them. Fostering a people-centric approach can present difficulties as it necessitates familiarity with a diverse range of individuals and active involvement in their interactions. In order to become an exceptional leader, it is imperative that you allocate sufficient time and exert considerable effort to acquaint yourself with your team members. Such a commitment is indispensable.

Show consideration for the needs of your members.

Exhibiting attentiveness to the requirements of your constituents entails possessing an understanding of their needs prior to them explicitly expressing them. Familiarize yourself thoroughly with your team members and evaluate their individual strengths and areas for improvement, enabling you to effectively provide them with appropriate guidance as and when required. It is equally important to exhibit sensitivity when observing instances of subpar performance or when individuals encounter challenges in fulfilling their responsibilities. It is incumbent upon you to ensure that they are motivated.

Have initiative

Mastering the art of taking initiative can prove to be a formidable challenge. Through your proactive approach, you will assume the role of guiding your subordinates in taking proactive measures and providing support in the decision-making process, particularly in situations where no other individuals are demonstrating leadership. It necessitates a perpetual state of preparedness, poised for action even prior to the exigency. By displaying proactive behavior, you can mitigate the likelihood of encountering setbacks and earn the admiration of your peers. Consequently, individuals will aspire to emulate your example, ensuring collective triumph in your respective performances and endeavors.

Take risks

A capable leader does not shy away from embracing risks. Indeed, there are numerous factors that necessitate careful consideration when embarking on ventures that involve risk-taking. Occasionally, the rewards may prove inadequate; however, it is through venturing into uncertain territory and pushing oneself beyond perceived limits that one can truly accomplish remarkable feats. Do not hesitate to partake in novel ventures and embrace unfamiliar pursuits. You may find it astonishing to witness the remarkable accomplishments that lie ahead for you and your team.

Be goal-oriented

In conclusion, it is imperative to consistently establish a clear objective. The proficiency and efficacy of a leader can solely be gauged based on his aptitude to execute the objectives he establishes. Having a strong sense of purpose entails that your actions are driven by a desire to achieve significant outcomes, rather than solely engaging in activities for the sake of doing them. It is imperative that you consistently align your actions and decisions with this objective.

By adhering to the aforementioned suggestions, one can cultivate the mindset and demeanor of a leader. Maintain cognizance of these factors and diligently monitor your advancement while cultivating and augmenting your aptitude for leadership.

Regarding the Comprehension and Manipulation of Others

Have you ever pondered the phenomenon in which two individuals engage in a conversation and subsequently interpret the discourse in divergent manners? Occasionally, we encounter situations where we participate in events alongside companions, only to engage in subsequent disagreements regarding the actual unfolding of those events. How is this possible? Throughout the course of the day, we are incessantly inundated with an uninterrupted stream of information, while our cerebral faculties are inherently restricted in their capacity to perceive and comprehend a given quantum of information concurrently. The process by which we choose information is predominantly unconscious and relies loosely on our preferred sensory perception. For instance, while one person may have a greater recollection of visual information, another person may have a superior recall of auditory information. To the best of one's recollection, meaning is constructed by the individual who undergoes the events. Every individual possesses their own distinctive method of information processing, and it is crucial for us to recognize and acknowledge this fact if we aspire to effectively comprehend one another.

The overwhelming majority of the information encountered throughout our daily activities tends to be disregarded or overlooked, and what remains is largely the information upon which we base our decision-making. After being accumulated, the information acquired throughout the day is subsequently subjected to our individual perspectives, encompassing political, cultural, social, and personal implications and conjectures. These interpretations stimulate our cognitive faculties, leading to subsequent impact on our affective states.

In order to comprehend others, it is necessary to engage in the process of reverse engineering their actions and emotions, thereby discerning their cognitive and emotional framework that influences their subjective understanding of events and intentions. By scrutinizing the conduct of others in such a manner, we can cultivate a more profound comprehension of the person's individual convictions and cognitive mechanisms.

Engaging with an individual's beliefs goes beyond being a merely persuasive strategy. The advantages are manifold, encompassing at least three distinct aspects:

A thorough comprehension fosters more profound connections and establishes trust.

You mitigate the possibility of misinterpretation.

A conviction is apt to motivate an individual towards proactive behavior.

In Business

Comprehending an organization is strikingly analogous to comprehending an individual. Currently, it is customary for companies to possess a documented set of principles, typically composed of popular buzz words. Based on these values, we can discern the organization's self-perception and desired external perception.

There exist two implicit inquiries that every company or individual invariably ponders upon while deliberating whether to engage in commerce with a particular organization:

Does this provide me with the impression that this offer is advantageous?

Am I favorably disposed towards the company/individual I am transacting with?

Your objective should be to affirmatively address both of these questions prior to their emergence. In order to accomplish this, an array of strategies and tactics can be utilized, with certain techniques being most effective in person, while others are more apt for telephone or email exchanges.

Negotiation Skills

A negotiation can be characterized as an engagement in which multiple parties adhere to predetermined guidelines with the intention of cultivating mutually advantageous circumstances. There exist guidelines that must be adhered to during negotiations lest the process devolves into chaos. The subsequent recommendations will significantly enhance your prospects of achieving success during the negotiation process.

Before engaging in any negotiations, it is advisable to position yourself at a slight angle from your counterpart, thus avoiding a direct face-to-face seating arrangement.

Ensure clarity regarding what holds significance.

Engage in a comprehensive analysis of the negotiation by treating it as a mutual challenge.

During the course of negotiations, it is advisable to focus on progressing towards desired objectives rather than getting sidetracked by attempts to merely avoid or solve problems.

If bestowed with an offer by someone, engage in a comprehensive discussion concerning the proposition, prior to proceeding or contemplating any form of counter offer.

In the context of negotiations, employ direct questioning rather than making declarative statements.

Upon the conclusion of the negotiation process, it is advised to provide a comprehensive summary encompassing all topics discussed and highlighting any advancements achieved. This will guarantee that there are no misunderstandings.

Integrity and Continuity

As individuals, the extent of our moral fiber and genuineness is predominantly assessed by the level of integrity we possess, or the integrity we are perceived to exhibit. Adhering to our obligations fosters integrity, dependability, and ultimately, contentment. Integrity is among the most invaluable qualities an individual can cultivate, in conjunction with intelligence, steadfastness, and resoluteness. There may come instances when your integrity is challenged and put to the test; these situations frequently serve as opportunities for shaping your character and should be approached with utmost seriousness.

The presence of honesty and integrity among team members will yield consistently superior outcomes. Establishing trust is of utmost significance within a team; it is imperative for you to provide ethical leadership to your team. Maintaining unwavering commitment to your promises becomes increasingly pivotal when confronted with periods of organizational transformation. Team leaders and managers, on occasion, may seek to control the dissemination of information to their team in order to safeguard them. However, this approach will inevitably prove detrimental, as it will erode the trust your team places in your credibility and leadership aptitude.

In the realm of corporate enterprises, the preservation of continuity inherently paves the path towards sustainability, hence rendering integrity as a pivotal component of a well-devised and impactful strategy. Meticulously crafted business plans exhibit a perceptible alignment with business policies and organizational structures from their inception, wherein the diverse factors are diligently evaluated in order of significance. After attaining establishment, it is crucial for a business to ensure the ongoing preservation of organizational continuity and integrity in order to effectively maneuver through the challenges of the corporate landscape. An ethical organization's meticulous assessment and strategic preparations will extend beyond the customary focus on compliance matters and health and safety considerations, as it aligns with both ethical imperatives and principles of morality to do so.

In order to preserve the integrity of the organization, it is imperative for businesses to implement a hybrid framework encompassing both formal and informal methodologies and procedures that adhere to legal requirements while also upholding the principles and ideals of the company. It is imperative that the values and processes be unambiguous, straightforward, and reflect the overarching ethical foundation shared among the employees.

It is important to bear in mind that it is preferable to decline a task rather than accept it without the ability to complete it promptly or comprehensively. In addition to upholding your promises, the ability to fulfill your commitments has a profound impact on the individuals in your vicinity. For instance, in the scenario where one is tasked with organizing an event and discovers 24 hours prior that the expected turnout will be relatively low, proceeding with the event would remain advantageous from a long-term perspective. It would carry significant importance for the individuals in attendance, while also upholding your integrity and preserving your sense of continuity.

Rapport

To establish a connection with an individual or group is to cultivate a symbiotic comprehension of thoughts and emotions, resulting in a seamless exchange of communication among the parties involved. The acquisition of strong rapport skills should be deemed imperative knowledge for individuals aspiring to achieve success in the professional realm. The establishment of a strong bond and admiration between individuals culminates in significant and enduring connections. Possessing efficient communication abilities is highly esteemed, and once established, a strong rapport will serve as a valuable asset in both personal and professional interactions. Numerous theoretical frameworks are devoted to acquiring and sustaining rapport, extending from NLP (Neuro Linguistic Programming) to employing psychological strategies in marketing, advertising, and even conventional cold calling scripts.

What strategies can be employed to establish and sustain rapport? There are several factors to contemplate prior to embarking on any endeavors to enhance the existing levels of rapport. The endeavor to employ strategies and approaches to establish a harmonious connection carries considerable risks and, if executed inadequately, can be transparent, thus giving the impression of being artificial. This will result in an outcome contrary to the intended effect, leading to a considerable decline in levels of rapport. In order to successfully apply acquired skills to organic interactions, it is imperative to possess a combination of self-assurance and proficiency. Optimal interactions are characterized by an inherent sense of spontaneity and effortless progression toward mutually advantageous outcomes. If your manner of communication lacks rapport, you will be regarded as monotonous, predictable, and potentially even impolite. Presented herewith are a series of proven techniques aimed at fostering rapport.

Managing Change Effectively

At one juncture or another, it is incumbent upon all individuals to acquire knowledge in the effective management of change. It is indeed a gratifying sentiment to possess a well-constructed blueprint for one's future endeavors. You might be pursuing a higher education at an academic institution, striving to earn a coveted degree; alternatively, you could be diligently accumulating funds with the aim of acquiring your envisaged dream residence. Regardless, you had not made any provisions for significant deviations in your life trajectory. The proficient administration of change may determine the divergent outcome of prospering amid such changes or experiencing disintegration due to an inability to adjust to alterations in established plans.

When confronted with an alteration in the trajectory leading towards the future, persisting in attachment to what was, can prove to be a significant impediment towards advancing. It is imperative that you pursue an alternative objective or explore a different approach to attaining it. Declining to embrace the change will likewise impede your capacity to envision the true manifestation of the future.

Cut out Negativity

An additional obstacle encountered by individuals when navigating change pertains to the presence of individuals who exhibit negativity. The challenge of countering the effects of individuals in your vicinity who resist change is nearly comparable to the struggle of overcoming such inclinations within yourself. Change management occasionally necessitates restricting your engagement with these individuals or entirely eliminating them from your social circle. This can prove to be a challenging circumstance, particularly when these individuals are your family members or intimate acquaintances. However, if they are unable to provide encouragement for your fresh perspective on life, they are impeding your progress.

Prepare for Changes

Certain changes may manifest abruptly, such as the onset of an illness or an unforeseen accident. However, one can enhance their preparedness for other changes by consistently evaluating their circumstances and adopting a proactive approach upon recognizing indications of impending change. In the event that one discerns indications of forthcoming change, endeavor to effectuate a corresponding adjustment. If altering it is not within your control, it would be prudent to make appropriate arrangements or gain a thorough comprehension of how effective change management can impact the result of a given scenario.

Channel Your Energy

Allowing oneself to be overwhelmed by a sense of injustice hinders the ability to channel one's energy towards the creation of a fresh objective. The alteration can be deemed as unjust; individuals of integrity succumb, fall ill, and face unemployment. Regrettably, the inherent inequity of a circumstance does not alleviate its repercussions; nevertheless, one's ability to navigate and embrace transformation can transmute an unjust occurrence into a fortuitous outcome. Numerous individuals perceive unforeseen adversities as inequitable due to a prevailing sense of entitlement, wherein they believe they are entitled to an idyllic existence. However, it is an inescapable reality that nearly every individual encounters circumstances that thwart their meticulously laid out aspirations. The manner in which you oversee and adapt to changes in your life ultimately determines how they shape your circumstances.

Rather than fixating on your losses and wishing for a return to the previous state, direct your attention towards your objective, how you will achieve it, and the novel approach through which you will reach your goal. Envision the realization of your objectives and maintain a focused mindset on the merits that await in the future, as opposed to harboring regrets over the occurrence of this transformation. It will prove to be challenging, as the initial endeavor of strategic future planning consisted of substantial difficulties, and this subsequent iteration is expected to present even greater obstacles. Prioritizing the initial stage is essential to readjusting your objectives and approaches in accordance with the prevailing circumstances.

Effective Change Management Involves Addressing and Mitigating Apprehension

The apprehension associated with unfamiliar circumstances poses an additional obstacle to successfully overseeing changes and reconfiguring life plans. There is a possibility of not attaining success. An integral aspect of experiencing gratification in accomplishing a goal lies in the sense of unpredictability experienced throughout the journey. Revising your plans may seem like a daunting decision due to the absence of assured success, yet it is highly probable that failure will ensue if you neglect to acknowledge and embark on exploring alternative approaches to achieve your objectives.

"Here are several guidelines that may assist you in effectively navigating through changes:

Expect change and be prepared for any outcome.
Continuously monitor changes and consistently assess your circumstances in order to avoid any sudden surprises resulting from any unexpected alterations.

Rapidly acclimate to change; investing valuable time in yearning for stability hinders progress towards fresh objectives.

Please bear in mind these recommendations for effectively navigating change, as circumstances may once again undergo alteration.

Implementing change can present challenges, yet acknowledging the magnitude of the endeavor may prove to be the most arduous aspect. Once you consciously embrace your new reality and relinquish fear of the transition and its management, you will experience a sense of well-being. Adeptly navigating change will present you with an enhanced opportunity to derive satisfaction from your life.

Key Factors Contributing to Achievement: Strategic Planning and Efficient Organization

The achievement of a leader is assured when they possess the ability to strategize and coordinate effectively. This chapter aims to provide instructions on achieving simplicity in the most straightforward manner. In addition, you will review select examples from the preceding chapter, such as the process of formulating SMART goals.

Regarding the aspect of planning and arranging, it is advisable to strategically plan the tasks at hand, ensuring that they are organized in accordance with their level of importance. It is ill-advised to invest effort into tasks that lack urgency or significance. We will present to you a singular illustration of a 'matrix' that can be utilized for the purpose of strategizing your objectives for the present day and beyond, taking into account their significance and immediacy.

Let us delve further into the topic of planning and organization.

Why is planning imperative?

Planning is crucial as it demands deliberate consideration and identification of the precise objectives one aims to attain. How do you plan to arrive at your destination? What challenges or obstacles do you anticipate encountering?

What strategies will you employ to address those challenges in the event that they occur? You desire utmost clarity and meticulousness in your planning. You are required to comprehend the specific actions that need to be implemented.

The absence of strategic planning, be it for the immediate or distant future, can lead to an array of complications. Additionally, it suggests making modifications in real-time should unforeseen circumstances arise.

The Eisenhower Matrix: Facilitating Prioritization and Streamlining Planning Utilizing the Eisenhower matrix is an outstanding approach to establishing your objectives, even if it is solely for a given day. It is compartmentalized into four discrete sectors (or quadrants). "It is formulated in the following manner: Pressing/Critical (Address immediately) Non-pressing/Yet Important (Arrange) Priority/Duty (Delegate) Non-urgent/Insignificant (Exclude)

As evident from the visual display, the tasks residing within the upper left quadrant necessitate immediate attention and therefore should be considered your foremost priorities. If there are tasks that require completion but you possess insufficient time, consider assigning them to an individual who is capable and available. Conversely, we have tasks of noteworthy importance that, although not immediately pressing, can be scheduled for a later time.

Ultimately, there are non-critical and non-significant tasks that must be relegated to a lower priority. Alternatively, they can be promptly eradicated. Please prioritize tasks within the Urgent/Important quadrant.

Imagine that your day is predominantly comprised of fulfilling time-sensitive obligations and participating in formal gatherings. You are currently engaged in a customer project that has an imminent deadline. The event is merely two days from now, and all indications suggest that things are progressing smoothly.

Irrespective of the extent of progress you have made, it would be illogical not to strategize beyond matters of immediate and significant concern. Suppose you are convening a meeting with your sales team. Although it is of utmost importance, it is not a catastrophic situation if it cannot be accomplished this morning.

Schedule it for a later time within the same day. It could potentially be arranged for a subsequent time later during the week. This shall be influenced by the volume of tasks allocated to you.

Then there's social media. This is the point at which matters start to grow a bit intricate. If you are using it for promotional purposes for your company, you may want to outsource it as it is a minor task that can be completed quickly.

The engagement in personal social media should be discouraged due to its propensity for causing distractions. Kindly await until the conclusion of the working hours. As evident from the presentation, the Eisenhower Matrix effectively amalgamates strategic planning and meticulous organization.

By incorporating this into your routine, you will effortlessly perform tasks, enhance your organizational skills, and significantly boost your productivity.

Organization = Creativity

An additional factor contributing to the significance of order is resourcefulness. An individual will be in need of your assistance in resolving a matter, and it is possible that you possess the means to help them. Moreover, the solution can be readily identified as you possess the information of its whereabouts.

Strategic resource allocation necessitates careful planning. One can discern its correct utilization by observing it in operation. And you will solely distribute it to the appropriate individuals.

It is additionally advantageous as it fosters resource preservation rather than resource wastage. Ascertain their nature and guarantee that upon distribution, they fall into the possession of individuals who will effectively utilize them. Additionally, it obviates the requirement to seek out a competent individual.

Always communicate.

Efficient communication plays a crucial role in the facilitation of planning and organization protocols. You establish objectives and arrange them based on priority. Examine the requisite urgency of expeditiously accomplishing a task as opposed to delaying it, and vice versa.

Ensure a consistent understanding among all stakeholders. If nobody is present, kindly inquire about the nature of the issue. Grant them the opportunity to expound upon the matter, thus enabling you to conduct a more comprehensive analysis.

When the execution of plans proceeds without the unanimous consent or agreement of all parties involved, the resulting consequences can be calamitous. This is the rationale behind the advantages derived from conducting periodic team meetings and check-ins. In this manner, you will have the opportunity to observe the progress made thus far and identify the remaining tasks that require attention.

This chapter has elucidated effective strategies for devising and arranging your daily schedule with a clear and systematic approach. It is possible to develop a comparable strategy that is centered on attaining your overarching goals. Every leader must possess the capacity to conceptualize and effectively arrange their objectives in order of importance.

You are required to promptly fulfill the specified objectives. It is imperative that you assign tasks to individuals who possess the necessary skills and abilities to successfully accomplish them. Simultaneously, it is necessary to make concessions in order to effectively regulate one's schedule and distribute it to prioritize tasks of significance.

Additionally, effective organization is necessary to prevent any wastage of resources. Moreover, effective communication will initiate the implementation of the plans. You and your team are required to promptly convene to discuss the necessary tasks.

The Honest Leader

Placing one's trust in an individual who engages in deceitful behavior is an arduous and potentially unattainable task. Individuals desire to rely on individuals whom they are confident will refrain from deceiving or ensnaring them into engaging in activities contrary to their volition. For this very reason, it is imperative that a leader upholds honesty." "The rationale behind this is why it is imperative for a leader to possess honesty." "The principle at hand necessitates that a leader exhibit honesty.

Demonstrating sincerity with your team exemplifies your professionalism, even in situations where conveying the truth may not be favorable. Hence, it is imperative for a leader to consistently uphold transparency. The team would greatly appreciate this gesture and consequently make a dedicated effort to enhance their performance. Furthermore, by exemplifying honesty as a cherished virtue within the team, it would foster an environment where all members are inspired to engage in equitable and truthful interactions with one another.

Exercise caution in differentiating between honesty and candidness. It is imperative to additionally recognize and duly acknowledge the social customs and norms of the individuals with whom you engage in conversation, as excessive forthrightness is frequently deemed impolite in numerous societies. Strive to achieve a harmonious equilibrium between your sincerity and your tact, as this is a defining characteristic of an exceptional leader.

How to Become One:

In order to embody integrity as a leader, it is imperative to endeavor towards genuine authenticity. Though it may present difficulties, embodying unwavering honesty and steadfastly upholding personal beliefs is the cornerstone of exceptional leadership. Adopt a daily commitment to integrity by incorporating the subsequent approaches into your mindset:

Fulfill your obligations conscientiously. If one makes a commitment, it is imperative to adhere to it diligently. The esteem of individuals can solely be achieved when they possess the certainty that you exemplify the qualities of steadfastness and reliability. An individual who shirks their responsibilities in challenging situations unquestionably lacks the qualities required to be deemed a truly exceptional leader. With that being stated, it is important to discern when it is appropriate to decline. If you possess absolute certainty that something exceeds the capabilities of yourself or your team, it is imperative to demonstrate honesty by acknowledging this fact, rather than assuming the responsibility and yielding subpar results.

Accepting responsibility for your shortcomings. Individuals who engage in deceptive practices exhibit a tendency to conceal their inadequacies, as they experience feelings of shame or vulnerability in relation to them. They would go so far as to jeopardize the well-being of their team in order to safeguard their own interests and evade any potential conflict. While it may prove challenging, endeavor to maintain honesty in communicating your own errors with the rest of the team. They will exhibit heightened consideration and deliver a greater level of respect towards you upon realizing your awareness of your transgressions and witnessing your earnest endeavors towards betterment.

Be tactful. Difficulties arise solely from an individual's excessive candor when inappropriate language is utilized to convey honesty. A diligent leader is someone who ensures that the feedback provided is constructive and will serve as a source of inspiration for individuals to strive for improvement. Outstanding leadership entails the capacity to tackle circumstances in a candid and disciplined manner, without permitting personal sentiments of anger to impede the forward advancement of one's team.

Finally, ensure that your message is communicated with precision to its intended recipients. Do not assume that the rest of the team possesses psychic abilities enabling them to discern passive-aggressive remarks and utilize them for self-improvement. One can provide specific feedback while preserving individuals' emotions by employing the sandwich approach, wherein positive aspects are acknowledged first, followed by constructive criticism, and concluding with additional positive feedback. This will enable you to uphold honesty while maintaining the morale of your team.

Exude positivity and provide heartfelt motivation

Despite possessing a clear vision and adept strategizing skills, the absence of effective motivation and encouragement towards one's followers to cultivate their fullest potential, exert diligent efforts, and uphold a shared objective, will present arduous challenges.

However, not all leaders possess the knowledge and skills to effectively serve as a motivating influence. Some individuals demand excessive efforts from their followers. Providing encouragement and backing in lieu of engaging in bullying tactics will secure the unwavering loyalty of your teams and contribute to the cultivation of a positive and esteemed leadership image. Consistently, there exists a correct manner in which to execute tasks.

Below are some guidelines to become a constructive influence for motivation:

Recognize the significance of collaborative efforts within a team setting. It would be incorrect to claim full credit for one's accomplishments when one is aware that others contributed to the attainment of their objective. If your team is aware of the recognition they receive and your proficiency in expressing gratitude towards them, they will reciprocate their appreciation towards you as well. Collaboration becomes hindered when a pervasive sense of animosity is present, thus it is imperative that mutual respect and appreciation be cultivated. In this manner, you can ensure that you will achieve optimal outcomes. Additionally, it is imperative to consistently acknowledge and commemorate the positive accomplishments that have transpired as a result of the collective efforts of your team and to duly attribute credit to those responsible.

One should continuously cultivate their dreams and strive to achieve further objectives. Naturally, attaining certain goals is a prerequisite before contemplating further aspirations; nevertheless, it is acceptable to entertain alternate plans and aspirations. Do not confine yourself to merely one category when you have the ability to expand your outreach and cater to a larger clientele.

Remember to follow up. In the event that a task is not expedited promptly, be diligent in initiating follow-up actions without necessitating your clients or customers to expressly request such. Have some initiative. In the event that a leader displays proactive tendencies, it is highly likely that their subordinates will align themselves and comprehend the notion that action can be taken without explicit instruction.

Listen. Do not solely engage in verbal communication and adopt an excessively didactic approach; instead, acquire the skill of actively listening to the insights and perspectives articulated by your team members. It is essential to recall that, as mentioned in a prior chapter, the process of brainstorming holds significant importance. It possesses immense efficacy and possesses the potential to facilitate the expansion of your organization. Gain wisdom through the reciprocal exchange of knowledge with others.

Have clear goals. There is no greater detriment than having a leader who lacks clarity in their objectives. Ensure that you have a precise understanding of your objectives, as this will enable your team to direct their attention towards them as well. Additionally, it is imperative to engage in open discussions with your team regarding the rationale behind your objectives. If individuals grasp the rationale behind the tasks they are required to perform, it is highly probable that their commitment, diligence, and endorsement will be secured.

Encourage your followers. Do not embody the type of leader who possesses an excessive sense of self-importance, to the extent that they fail to acknowledge their subordinate's crucial role in their own achievements. Consistently express your belief in their abilities, affirming your confidence in their potential to achieve remarkable accomplishments. Emphasize that through collaborative efforts, opportunities for tremendous achievements can be realized by each individual involved. Encourage and motivate them instead of admonishing them, and you will witness a noticeable improvement leading to a more relaxed and straightforward experience for everyone involved.

Encourage them to step outside of their comfort zones, while also pushing yourself to do the same. Do not restrict yourself to mediocrity when you are capable of achieving excellence. Encourage individuals to critically examine their thought processes and embrace the opportunity to acquire knowledge in areas they may be unfamiliar with. Once more, do not hesitate to undertake ventures and instill in your team the belief that they possess the capacity to achieve greater and more significant accomplishments beyond their current knowledge and abilities.

Be enthusiastic. To instill a strong work ethic and foster a sense of purpose among your subordinate employees, display sincere enthusiasm for your work and the collective efforts of your team. Please refrain from arriving at the workplace while experiencing persistent fatigue. This will have an impact on all individuals in your vicinity. Maintain a sense of enthusiasm towards your work, and as a result, you will be capable of generating more significant outcomes. Establishing a conducive atmosphere will yield positive outcomes, thereby aligning with the desired objective.

Exercise vigilance in addressing the needs and demands of your followers. It would be inappropriate to solely request your team to exert effort without inquiring about their needs or ascertaining their comfort level regarding the tasks assigned to them. It is imperative to keep in mind that, as a cohesive unit, it is essential to display genuine concern and regard for one another. A proficient leader is not merely an individual who delegates tasks and responsibilities to their team, but rather someone who is able to cultivate meaningful bonds and companionship as well. Ensure the well-being of your team members so that they may reciprocate in kind.

Furthermore, refrain from imposing tasks upon your followers which you are unwilling to undertake yourself. If one were unable to engage in a leap from the pinnacle of a structure devoid of any protective measures underneath, why then would one request their adherents to undertake such perilous actions? Be fair. Merely holding a position of authority does not necessitate employing that power in an oppressive manner towards subordinates. You will fail to garner respect and admiration if you exhibit a hunger for power and a lack of concern for those in your surroundings.

In order to serve as a constructive source of motivation, it is imperative to possess a positive demeanor. Despite potential changes in the world, the possession of strong values and ideals remains irreplaceable, and a competent leader should indeed embody such traits.

Planning

Effective management is characterized by meticulous planning. Properly strategizing is crucial in order to circumvent impulsive responses to events and circumstances. Through the process of strategic planning, managers are able to gain comprehensive insights into the intricacies of the task at hand, effectively relay pertinent information to the team, and cultivate a proactive outlook for the project. Presented below are essential components of effective planning that a competent manager must ensure.

Goal-setting.

It is imperative for the manager to establish a precise objective for which the planning exercise is being undertaken. There may exist multiple objectives on the horizon, however, it is advisable to strategize one objective at a time, in order to prevent any confusion amidst the goals and the personnel entrusted with their fulfillment. These objectives can be classified as "short-term" and "long-term" goals. Short-term goals typically refer to those that require implementation within a few months, whereas long-term goals are characterized by later deadlines.

Deadlines.

Establish concrete timelines for each objective. The establishment of deadlines necessitates consideration of the feasibility of the established timeframe. Namely, whether the objective can be attained within the specified timeframe. The evaluation of a deadline's feasibility and attainability is contingent upon numerous factors, including the prompt availability of essential resources, unpredictable weather patterns such as rain or snow, uninterrupted access to electricity, and the occurrence of holiday seasons, among others. If the established deadline is unattainable, appropriate actions must be taken to rectify the situation. Additional personnel need to be allocated to the task, or it is necessary to notify the client that an adjustment to the deadline is necessary. Personnel are typically equipped to operate effectively in high-pressure situations, yet it would be inequitable to anticipate them to consistently meet abrupt time constraints. This situation reflects poorly on the manager, indicating a lack of diligence in setting goals with his superiors.

Break up the goal.

Engaging in a discourse regarding a high-level objective tends to evoke apprehension among individuals. A June announcement regarding the release of a film in December is expected to significantly elevate everyone's stress levels. However, dividing the identical objective into smaller objectives and establishing bimonthly or monthly deadlines instills a sense of ease among all individuals involved. The macro announcement is expected to elicit skepticism and apprehension, whereas the subsequent approach of breaking down the primary objective into smaller milestones generates a sense of enthusiasm among the personnel for the project. The proclamation of a significant objective does not instill a sense of personal responsibility; however, by devising smaller objectives, the personnel assigned to each respective goal can assume ownership of it.

Resource allocation.

Effective planning entails careful consideration of the individuals responsible for specific tasks and the manner in which these tasks are to be carried out. This encompasses the distribution of expertise, manpower, and machinery. In certain instances, the current personnel within the department may lack the requisite skills to effectively carry out a specific objective. Consequently, the manager would need to request the assistance of competent personnel from alternative departments, external sources, or consider outsourcing the specific task. The essence of the concept lies in the strategic assignment of individuals best suited for the task at hand, regardless of its nature. Similarly with physical resources. Effective planning entails creating a comprehensive inventory encompassing all necessary equipment and accessories for the project's execution. It is not uncommon for resources to become depleted during the course of the project, resulting in unproductive periods until the resources are replenished. This situation poses a significant drawback for the company as it leads to avoidable escalation of costs. This occurrence is frequently witnessed in the domain of public infrastructure projects, wherein a venture experiences an unexpected culmination owing to an abrupt cessation of essential resources.

Anticipate bottlenecks.

An indication of effective management is the ability to proactively predict obstructions and make sufficient arrangements to address them, rather than attempting to resolve them reactively during their occurrence. It is rare for a project to proceed without any hitches; it is inevitable that bottlenecks will arise. A proficient manager, leveraging both his own expertise and that of his team, will possess the foresight to anticipate a multitude of these situations and accordingly establish appropriate measures. Nevertheless, notwithstanding your diligent attempts to foresee and prepare for potential hindrances, certain unforeseeable circumstances may arise, such as a cyclone or a warehouse fire, which could not have been predicted by anyone. These adverse bottlenecks necessitate innovative thinking on the part of the manager to eliminate.

Leadership Attributes Pertaining to Decision-Making and Crisis Management

As a leader, it is imperative to consistently maintain contingency plans for all endeavors. In the event that you lack an alternative course of action, you may encounter considerable challenges in managing the severe repercussions stemming from your choices. Presented below are several crucial attributes inherent in effective leadership that prove particularly invaluable during challenging periods, notably concerning the facilitation of difficult choices and adept crisis management.

Quality 1 - Intuition

When guiding a team through uncharted or unfamiliar territories, typically there is an absence of a definitive guide delineating the course of action or path to be pursued. There is a lack of clarity in every aspect, and in such instances, the burden of expectations can become overwhelming. In the midst of traversing unfamiliar territories, a leader must rely on their inherent intuition. It is incumbent upon you to provide guidance to your team throughout the course of your regular activities. On occasion, there may be uncertainty in one's mind, yet it becomes necessary to place reliance upon both one's intuition and the abilities of team members. Subsequently, in the event of novel occurrences and the subsequent emergence of unforeseen circumstances, your team will undoubtedly seek your guidance.

When confronted with a crisis, it is vital to apply the lessons derived from past experiences in order to inform decision-making. In due course, however, arduous circumstances shall subside, and one shall inevitably derive valuable lessons from such situations. You must rely on your innate intuition to discern the correct solutions. In the event that an error has been made, it is imperative to derive valuable lessons from it, thus enabling its transformation into a constructive learning opportunity for application in future endeavors. It is imperative to maintain faith in oneself. It is crucial to place great importance on one's own trust and decision-making capabilities when endeavoring to gain the confidence and trust of one's team.

Quality 2 - Creativity

Exceptional leaders often exhibit innovative thinking beyond conventional boundaries. They possess the ability to perceive the broader perspective and transcend traditional norms. They consistently possess an alternative option, an additional selection, or a contingency plan. Exhibiting creative tendencies serves as a crucial attribute for effective leadership. It is of significant assistance in not only crafting optimal decisions, but also in selecting a resolution for a problem that would yield the most favorable outcome.

In times of crisis or unforeseen circumstances, the majority of your team will turn to you and rely on your guidance and judgement. Therefore, it is imperative to exercise resourcefulness and ingenuity in the process of making strategic choices. Your decision must exhibit both effectiveness and ingenuity. Acquire the skill of carefully evaluating circumstances and refrain from making hasty judgments.

Criterion 3 - Aptitude for Wit and Humor

Whilst not obligatory, staff members tend to exhibit a greater preference for a charismatic and amiable leader who fosters a positive and relaxed professional atmosphere, as opposed to a severe and inflexible manager. As it is incumbent upon you to cultivate a positive atmosphere within your professional setting, engaging in lighthearted banter would undoubtedly prove efficacious. According to studies conducted, individuals tend to acquire a greater amount of knowledge when information or ideas are conveyed in a humorous manner.

The act of laughter triggers the release of hormones that induce a sense of well-being, thereby facilitating the assimilation of information by an individual. This phenomenon is also observed in the context of your professional environment. By implementing measures to enhance the ambiance, it is probable that the productivity of your employees will be augmented. Any form of pressure will not be amplified. Attaining your team objective would be facilitated by ensuring a positive working environment for all team members.

Strategic Approaches to Leadership in the Management of Millennials: Transforming the Singular Approach into a Tailored Strategy.

Adapting your leadership and management approach to meet the needs of the Millennial generation while effectively communicating your objectives and expectations is a gradual process that cannot be accomplished hastily. It necessitates the undertaking of several measures that enable effective leadership of millennial individuals and maximizing their potential.

The initial phase of this procedure entails modifying your approach of employing a universal strategy that caters to all individuals.

A study has revealed that Millennials harbor dissatisfaction towards the utilization of the prevalent 'one size fits all' method by baby boomers. Employers hailing from the Baby Boomer and Generation X cohorts are of the opinion that a singular approach or system is universally effective, whereby a stimulus that motivates a particular group of workers will automatically inspire the remainder of the workforce.

Millennials demonstrate a disinclination towards this approach and assert that the present working model necessitates revisions and modifications to align with the unique requirements of individual employees. A primary factor contributing to the lack of synergy and productivity between Millennials and Baby Boomers stems from the prevailing expectation among the latter for the former to adhere rigidly to established customs and traditions.

In order to enhance ease and productivity in dealing with your millennial workforce, it is essential to refrain from employing a generic approach and instead embrace the following methods to ensure engagement and job satisfaction among the Generation Y employees.

Consistently evaluate the employee's performance

In order to effectively address the management of millennial employees, it is essential to regularly evaluate their performance, thereby gaining insights into their individual work styles.

Provide Regular Feedback

Once you have evaluated the work accomplished by employees from the millennial generation, promptly offer feedback. Keep in mind, the millennial demographic does not possess a penchant for enduring lengthy delays; they possess a strong desire to promptly enhance their work. In order to optimize the utilization of their energy, promptly provide them with what they are seeking.

When furnishing the feedback, incorporate comprehensive lists of tasks to inform them of their specific obligations. Furthermore, provide ample and insightful assistance and guidance concerning areas in which they have erred, while also acknowledging and commending their endeavors if they devise something creative and effective. Millennials have a strong desire for recognition; ensure that it is bestowed upon them.

Secondly, it would be beneficial to adopt a more compassionate and open approach when engaging with the millennial demographic. If they are unable to meet your expectations, it could be attributed to their ingenuity in generating novel concepts. Engage in a conversation with them to ascertain their perceptions. It is probable that their notion possesses merit and would benefit from your professional counsel to refine it.

Moreover, when delivering feedback to the Millennial generation, engage in comprehensive discussion to eliminate any potential ambiguity or misinterpretation. Given the divergent cognitive frameworks between yourself and the millennial generation, it is evident that your perception of information also varies. Through engaging in a conversation about the appraisal, you articulate your perspective and ensure that their actions align with the anticipated norms.

Accept their Ideas

It is imperative that you begin to cultivate a mindset that is receptive to novel and unconventional concepts as well. If you hold the belief that establishing an electronic commerce platform is dispensable in facilitating the expansion of your business, it is worth considering the perspective of your marketing manager who belongs to the Millennial generation. In the event that adequate financial resources are available to substantiate this notion, it would be prudent to embark upon this venture and subsequently appraise the subsequent progress and development of the enterprise. There is a high probability that their concept will prove advantageous for your enterprise.

Conduct Seminars and Workshops

Organize conferences and training sessions that feature seasoned executives, analysts, and entrepreneurs engaging in dialogue with millennial and Baby Boomer employees. This facilitates the exposure of both generations to novel ideas and diverse working methodologies.

You are instructed to delegate authority to the middle management

Rather than solely allocating full authority to the senior management, it is advisable to establish an intermediate management layer responsible for evaluating the work and performance of employees, providing regular updates and insights to the top management. It is imperative for them to conduct separate evaluations of each employee and refrain from making comparisons between them. Furthermore, it is imperative for employees to possess a requisite level of autonomy in order to exercise their judgement and foster a sense of empowerment and significance within the organization. This guarantees that no employee is limited to a single approach, thus ensuring that all employees embrace diverse methodologies in order to achieve the desired outcome.

By implementing these strategies, you will be able to effectively oversee your millennial workforce. After completing this task, you may proceed to implement the subsequent approach.

Develop the qualities that make a leader highly effective.

Your attributes are what ultimately encompass your effectiveness as a leader. No individual, regardless of gender, has ever succeeded in any form of leadership role, be it through election or appointment, without possessing the qualities that we will delve into momentarily.

Herein lie the essential leadership qualities one must possess prior to acquiring the self-assurance necessary to effectively guide or exert influence over others:

Live with Integrity

Exhibiting unwavering integrity, even in the absence of observation, constitutes the fundamental cornerstone of embodying true leadership. Integrity refers to one's capacity to uphold principles of honesty and fairness consistently across interactions with individuals in positions of authority, subordinates, colleagues, customers, competitors, government representatives, and others. Undeniably, integrity stands as a paramount characteristic crucial for leadership, regardless of one's present role or standing. Regardless of your position within the hierarchical structure of the company, possessing unwavering integrity will consistently prove advantageous in the long-term.

An individual with high moral principles neither welcomes bribes nor engages in blending personal and professional matters. There is no necessity to enumerate explicitly the matters of correct conduct and errors as they are already widely understood by all. The distinguishing factor between individuals of integrity and those devoid of this virtue lies in the unwavering commitment of the former to consistently opt for righteous courses of action. Despite its complexity. Despite the potential ramifications involved, akin to the situation faced by Maximus in the film Gladiator.

A leader is consistently committed to maintaining impeccable communication, expressing genuine intentions and ensuring accountability by aligning their words with corresponding actions. People perceive you as trustworthy due to the reputation you have diligently established.

A leader refrains from participating in office gossip and instead endeavors to mitigate such detrimental behaviors within the group.

One of the gravest implications for a leader is experiencing a deterioration of integrity, as it constitutes the fundamental cornerstone of effective leadership. Without upholding the virtue of integrity and instilling trust in others, one will encounter considerable challenges when attempting to exert influence or coordinate a collective of individuals.

Principle of Leadership #1: Cultivate a reputation for unwavering integrity in all circumstances, ensuring that your words consistently match your actions and fostering an environment of trust and dependability. This entails exemplifying integrity and impartiality in every circumstance, fulfilling one's commitments promptly and as promised.

Valuable Leadership Advice #2: Refrain from participating in any detrimental conduct, and if feasible, endeavor to intervene when confronted with others engaging in such behavior (provided it does not jeopardize your own well-being).

Take Responsibility

A genuine leader refrains from assigning blame when circumstances turn unfavorable. One cannot aspire to be a proficient and esteemed leader if they cannot endure and handle challenging circumstances when events deviate from the intended course.

A leader will perceive failure as a valuable learning experience, allowing them to enhance their leadership skills and prevent future occurrences of such failures.

Leadership Suggestion #3 Take responsibility for your own errors. In the majority of instances, displaying an eagerness to acquire knowledge from one's errors garners greater admiration compared to offering justifications for the failure or, even worse, shifting the blame onto another individual. As the leader of a team, the significance of assuming accountability for a failure is amplified, as the effectiveness of a team is solely dependent on its leader. Therefore, shifting blame will merely validate your inadequate leadership abilities.

Maintain Clearly Stated Objectives and Strategies

Exemplary leaders invariably exhibit a penchant for meticulous strategizing. If one aspires to maximize achievements within a constrained duration, it becomes imperative to cultivate precise objectives. How can one effectively guide others if they lack a clear understanding of the desired destination? In the absence of a clearly defined objective, how can a team operate with optimal efficiency and effectiveness?

Leadership Recommendation #4: Document your objectives. Should you aspire to assume a leadership role within your organization but have not yet achieved it, documenting your professional objectives will serve as evidence to your superiors of your determination, ambition, and existing leadership aptitude.

If you presently hold a position of leadership and do not possess clearly defined and documented objectives for both yourself and your team, it is imperative that you promptly undertake this task.

Engage in the act of openly communicating and discussing your objectives with your team members, while also fostering an environment that motivates them to reciprocate. Ensure that you encourage your team members to incorporate any professional development objectives they may have. In order to ensure enduring and impactful leadership, it is imperative that the objectives of your team extend beyond merely serving you and the organization, as there ought to be advantages and rewards for all stakeholders. Make a valuable contribution towards assisting your teammates in achieving their individual objectives whenever possible. When your team observes your genuine concern for their welfare, they will be more inclined to willingly contribute their efforts towards assisting you in achieving the objective. In numerous instances, they will provide an amount exceeding your initial expectations.

Developing clearly defined and documented objectives will instill trust and inspire confidence in your leadership capabilities, as it will demonstrate your strategic vision and direction. Nevertheless, simply being aware of your destination is insufficient; it is imperative that you possess the knowledge of the route to reach it. This is the point at which strategic planning becomes essential.

Leadership Pointer #5 Develop a comprehensive strategy. Once you have ascertained the underlying objective, it is advisable to devise a strategic approach encompassing practical measures that will pave the way towards achieving said objective.

Plans provide guidance on the appropriate actions to be taken at each juncture to avoid any time wastage. By establishing and adhering to strategic plans aimed at achieving your objectives, you will be able to assess your advancement and discern which strategies have been effective and which have not. This in turn enables you to make necessary modifications to the plans. Per the commonly held maxim, "that which can be quantified and assessed is more likely to demonstrate improvement."

To effectively set goals, it is essential to exhibit precision. Instead of expressing a desire to enhance sales, it is crucial to specify the exact magnitude by which you seek to raise them. Furthermore, articulate a clear and detailed plan outlining the sequential steps you intend to undertake in order to attain this goal, and ensure that you diligently take action towards its achievement on a daily basis.

As a leader, it is advisable to motivate your team by providing incentives for successfully achieving predetermined goals outlined within the plans.

Be Respectful

In the realm of leadership, the significance of respect cannot be overstated. In order to earn respect, it is essential to demonstrate respect. Individuals who experience a sense of esteem are more inclined to voluntarily adhere. In the event they are unable to identify any aspect deserving their respect in you, it becomes arduous to exert influence upon them in order to garner their compliance.

Regrettably, the majority of individuals in authoritative positions hold the belief that they are the sole recipients of respect solely by virtue of their occupational status. This is a contributing factor as to why certain leaders are unable to encourage maximum productivity among their subordinates.

Leadership Tip #6 Cultivate an atmosphere of respect. Respect is reciprocal. As a leader, it is imperative to demonstrate profound respect for and a willingness to embrace the diverse attributes and unique qualities of those within your sphere of influence. Approach differences in ideologies, religious beliefs, and political perspectives with tact and empathy, and you will earn the esteem of those you lead. When people feel like valued individuals their devotion to you will deepen.

Be Receptive

As a leader, it is imperative that you possess receptiveness towards novel ideas, a willingness to learn, and a thirst for knowledge. An individual tree is insufficient to constitute a forest. As a result, it is imperative that you remain receptive to guidance, feedback, recommendations, and insights provided by those in your vicinity. Should you assume the role of a leader who harbors the conviction that they possess all the necessary resources for success, thereby negating the need for assistance or attentiveness to the perspectives of those under your guidance, you shall inevitably steer towards failure.

Leadership Principle #7 Cultivate receptiveness and a willingness to consider diverse perspectives. Authentic leaders recognize that wisdom can be derived from individuals of all walks of life, irrespective of their societal standing. Although an individual may hold a subordinate position or possess lesser educational attainment, it should not be assumed that they lack valuable contributions to offer. Embrace the suggestions of others, particularly those under your leadership, and you will be regarded as a sagacious individual, earning profound respect. Instead of arrogantly dismissing ideas that do not originate from your own mind, adopt an inclusive approach that acknowledges diverse perspectives. While you possess extensive expertise in your domain, it is plausible that a junior colleague under your guidance might possess a deeper understanding in a subject matter that you are unfamiliar with.

Be Passionate

Few things propel success more swiftly than a relentless fervor. As an individual in a position of leadership, it is crucial to exhibit a profound enthusiasm and dedication to the objectives that have been established. Achieving success and exemplifying effective leadership necessitates such fervor.

Having a strong passion for your work will contribute to a heightened level of dedication and commitment to every project you embark upon. Passion increases your enthusiasm. Passionate leaders possess the charm required to instill a sense of purpose among team members and motivate them to actively pursue shared objectives.

Leadership Recommendation #8: Exhibit unwavering enthusiasm and effectively convey this enthusiasm to others.

Having established objectives, one finds it significantly simpler to cultivate a genuine enthusiasm for their professional responsibilities. Exemplify that passion on a daily basis and serve as a source of inspiration to those in your vicinity. Facilitate the discovery of individuals' enthusiasm for their occupations by ensuring widespread recognition of the indispensability of each job to the organization's seamless operation. Frequently, employees stray from the overarching objective and begin to experience a sense of diminished worth. When there is a shared understanding among individuals regarding their collective objectives and the significance of their respective roles in accomplishing those objectives, individuals can once again derive satisfaction from their professional responsibilities.

As a leader, it is imperative for you to consistently reinforce to your team the crucial role they fulfill within the organization. Demonstrate gratitude towards them and conduct yourself with a demeanor of enthusiasm, which increases the likelihood of reigniting the passion for their work among your team members.

If one finds themselves unable to cultivate genuine enthusiasm and zeal for their professional pursuits, regardless of holding a position of authority or not, it may be prudent to entertain the notion of pursuing an alternative vocation. If you lack genuine passion for your objectives, mobilizing others to work under your leadership will prove to be a challenging endeavor.

Be a Good Communicator

If one lacks proficient communication skills, it becomes exceedingly challenging to exert enduring favorable influence upon the individuals under one's leadership. Effective communication encompasses more than just having the knowledge of what to say and when to say it. It requires the ability to decipher and interpret the body language of those you are communicating with, as well as mastering the art of using your own body language to convey your message effectively.

Enhancing your proficiency as a leader necessitates further refinement of your listening abilities to optimize your communication effectiveness. Effective leaders possess the ability to actively engage in attentive listening, thus emphasizing the paramount significance of providing an empathetic ear to their followers without disregarding its value in any circumstance.

Leadership Tip #9 Endeavor to excel as a proficient communicator. Engage in active listening, inquire about the information shared to demonstrate comprehension, seek clarification when uncertainties arise, and interpret non-verbal cues to effectively understand the individual's emotions and adapt accordingly.

Be Self-Disciplined

As a person occupying a leadership role, it is imperative that you dedicate considerable effort towards obtaining this highly significant characteristic. A genuine leader will consistently set a precedent through their own actions. As an aspiring leader, it is imperative that you conduct yourself in a manner that commands respect and serves as an exemplary model for others, regardless of whether you are within the bounds of the professional sphere or beyond. Being a true leader entails embodying the qualities and principles of leadership, rather than merely fulfilling a set number of working hours each day.

While you may possess exceptional professional skills, engaging in excessive drinking or participating in questionable activities during weekends will significantly undermine your credibility, potentially resulting in the loss of valuable opportunities and the respect of your peers. Maintaining the respect of others is crucial for effective leadership.

Practical advice for effective leadership: Embodiment of exemplary behavior is essential. Possessing self-restraint is equivalent to possessing self-discipline. Exercise restraint over your emotions and exercise self-discipline in your actions. As a leader, it is imperative that you display composure and refrain from losing your temper, shouting, demeaning individuals, or partaking in behaviors that you would not want your team members to engage in. To gain the admiration of others, it is imperative that you exhibit composure, poise, and reasoned judgment when faced with various circumstances, so as to present yourself as an influential and revered leader. If one lacks the ability to exercise self-control, it raises doubts about their capacity to successfully guide and oversee others.

And should your level of self-control also encompass aspects of well-being and physical conditioning, it would be exceedingly beneficial. It will solely contribute to enhancing your reputation as an individual known for their unwavering principles, self-control, and admiration. When an individual maintains a sense of self-respect, it consequently heightens the likelihood of others displaying respect towards them, admiring their character, and ultimately emulating their guidance.

Value Time

Every esteemed leader comprehends the significance of time. You are unlikely to effectively exert a positive influence on your peers if you consistently exhibit disorganization and fail to meet deadlines regularly. The individuals who have achieved considerable success are aware that time is infinitely more precious than money, given the transient nature of financial resources. This understanding underscores the significance of optimizing one's use of time, as it cannot be recovered once lost. Do you ever experience the sensation that the duration of a single day appears to be insufficient? It is likely that the reason behind this issue is your lack of effective time management.

Leadership Tip # 11 Demonstrate the importance of effective time management through your own actions.

Efficiently leverage your agenda (assuming you possess one; if not, it is highly recommended to acquire one immediately!). Objectives ought to be delineated across intervals of one year, three months, and one month, subsequently further subdivided while strategizing weekly and daily plans. Allocate a few moments the evening prior to inscribe in your schedule the tasks you intend to achieve on the following day. Afterwards, proceed to allocate time for the completion of various tasks scheduled for the day.

Guidance for Effective Leadership #12: Avoid attempting to juggle multiple tasks simultaneously. While it may create the illusion of increased productivity, engaging in multitasking ultimately leads to a decrease in actual output, as well as a lack of focused and deliberate effort towards the task at hand.

Devote specific periods throughout the day to address incoming communications, such as emails and phone calls, rather than allowing constant disruptions from every phone call or email notification.

Naturally, it is imperative to remain adaptable in the unlikely event of an actual emergency transpiring; however, for the majority of circumstances, it is recommended to adhere to your predetermined schedule. Upon implementation of this practice, you will inevitably perceive a notable increase in the level of productivity throughout your day, along with the seemingly miraculous emergence of additional time at your disposal, in stark contrast to the haphazard approach of merely responding reactively to sudden occurrences.

Acquaint yourself with the Significance of Non-Verbal Communication

In addition to acquiring verbal communication skills, it is crucial to recognize that non-verbal communication plays a pivotal role in facilitating mutual understanding among individuals and ensuring effective leadership.

It is often said that actions carry more weight than words, emphasizing the significance of discerning the emotions of those around you through non-verbal interaction, such as interpreting their facial expressions and body language. An exemplary leader and proficient communicator is an individual who possesses the ability to skillfully utilize visual cues and symbols, requiring no explicit verbal explanation to comprehend the ongoing situation.

If one possesses adept non-verbal communication skills, the following outcomes could potentially transpire:

Complementing. Individuals may express their approval for your ability to effectively convey information to them and may offer compliments regarding your appearance or the manner in which you articulate your thoughts.

Contradiction. In actuality, it is not a negative occurrence. When individuals voice contrary perspectives or opinions, it indicates that your statement is logical and open to discussion. And in such instances, one can be assured of their capacity to exert influence over others, as it is evident that those individuals genuinely value the information imparted.

Repetition. They possess the ability to disseminate the information you have just conveyed, guaranteeing a wide reach and ensuring effective communication to a substantial audience.

Conversely, in the event that one lacks proficiency in non-verbal communication, there is potential for the occurrence of substitution. This situation entails the possibility of individuals incorrectly disseminating information about you or conveying a divergent message to others due to a lack of comprehension regarding your intended meaning. Consequently, it is imperative that you exercise caution in your choice of words and actions.

The various categories of Non-Verbal Communication encompass the following:

Gestures. Nonverbal cues provide clear indicators of a person's emotions or intended messages, even in the absence of spoken communication. Instances of physical actions that indicate communication include the act of indicating a direction or location, making a waving motion, or employing one's fingers to count or convey information pertaining to another individual's activities. Additionally, it would be prudent to further acquaint yourself with the diverse customs and gestures exhibited by individuals of varying cultural backgrounds.

Facial expressions. It is evident that a person's satisfaction with their current activities can be discerned through their facial expressions, and one would need to possess a considerable lack of sensitivity to be oblivious to such signals. One can discern various emotions, such as happiness, sarcasm, anger, sadness, frustration, and a wide range of other sentiments, by observing the facial expressions of an individual.

Eye gazing. According to popular belief, the inability to make direct eye contact suggests a lack of honesty. Although it may not be universally applicable, it is generally advantageous to maintain direct eye contact with individuals during conversation. This behavior signifies a genuine effort to capture their attention and conveys a sense of earnestness in discussing the matter at hand. Directly make eye contact with an individual, and it will swiftly capture their undivided attention.

Appearance. One's manner of self-presentation holds significant importance in interpersonal interactions. The manner in which you style your hair, select your attire, and apply cosmetics can convey significant insights into your personality, or rather, the persona you aim to present. As a leader, it is imperative that you maintain a professional appearance and refrain from any semblance of untidiness. It is imperative to ensure that an appropriate amount of makeup is applied, avoiding both excessive and insufficient application. Cultivate qualities that are deserving of emulation and admiration, and you will undoubtedly garner attention and captivate others.

Posture and Body Language. Actions such as crossing one's arms, casually flipping one's hair, or placing a hand on the waist are representative illustrations of body language. Expressions and emotions can be communicated through the aforementioned actions and also through an individual's body position. When an individual maintains upright posture, they tend to gain greater respect from others compared to individuals who slouch or portray an uncertain demeanor. Your demeanor carries substantial weight in reflecting your character and holds significant sway in shaping your public image.

Para-linguistics. This pertains to the manner in which one modulates their voice, including tone, pitch, and inflection. The manner in which one communicates will invariably undergo thorough analysis; therefore, it is imperative to exercise caution, deliberating upon the mode of delivery before expressing oneself. Occasionally, despite having good intentions, ineffective communication can hinder one's ability to be heard and understood by others. An effective leader possesses the ability to captivate and command the attention of individuals, ensuring that their words are conveyed with utmost precision.

Proximity. This denotes the spatial separation existing between yourself and the individual with whom you are engaged in conversation. Indeed, it would be advantageous to position yourself in proximity to an individual when seeking to facilitate a successful transaction or capture their attention. It is important, however, to exercise caution in this regard, ensuring that the proximity maintained is not overly intrusive or discomforting, particularly when engaging with someone of a different gender. It would also be prudent to communicate with utmost proficiency and effectiveness to maximize the desired outcome of the interaction. You would undoubtedly achieve exemplary outcomes by pursuing this course of action.

Recall, a fundamental aspect of exhibiting exceptional leadership involves effectively communicating with individuals. If one possesses the ability to engage in verbal communication, it is expected that they also possess the ability to engage in non-verbal communication.

Incremental Progress

Approach your life with diligence by directing your attention to singular tasks sequentially. This pertains not merely to your agenda, but also to the environment in which you find yourself. It is effortless to simultaneously open multiple tabs on the computer screen while attending to a phone call and viewing a film on your tablet. The abundance of external stimuli can pose challenges when it comes to effectively completing tasks. You tend to display a high susceptibility to distraction, which often leads to simultaneous engagement in multiple tasks rather than focusing on one activity at a time. Devote your entire attention to a single undertaking. You will achieve a more expedient completion and yield a superior final outcome. This approach enables increased productivity within a given day.

Acquiring the skill of organizing your thoughts can significantly enhance both your physiological and psychological health. The presence of excessive mental disarray can result in heightened exhaustion and uncontrollable outbursts of emotions. Employ multiple or all of the aforementioned techniques to facilitate the organization of your thoughts. Should you encounter any difficulty with one method, there is no cause for concern. However, maintaining perseverance is highly advised. Every individual possesses unique characteristics, thus implying that what proves effective for some individuals may not yield the same outcome for others. Upon discovering a suitable approach, adhere to it consistently, and witness the enhancement of your overall lifestyle.

Excessive rumination is an additional occurrence that obstructs cognitive functioning. Overanalyzing is characterized by repetitively dwelling on the same thought. Consideration may be given to an individual, a interpersonal connection, or an event that has exerted a substantial influence on your life. Excessive pondering can give rise to feelings of unease, melancholy, or heightened tension. Each of those disorders has an impact on your interpersonal relationships, capacity to maintain employment, financial well-being, and overall quality of life.

If one finds themselves engaging in excessive rumination, it is imperative to seek means of interrupting this cognitive pattern. Outlined below are several strategies to mitigate the propensity for excessive rumination.

Cease directing your attention towards negative possibilities.

It is quite effortless to succumb to the mentality wherein one envisions a multitude of unfavorable outcomes unfolding in one's life. Living in such a manner entails a highly pessimistic outlook. When one perceives the potential of an unfavorable outcome, it is highly probable that such perception shall be realized. This phenomenon can be referred to as a self-fulfilling prophecy. It signifies the ability to bring forth a conceptualization into actuality through the power of imagination. This phenomenon has the potential to operate in reverse. If one maintains an optimistic perspective, it is likely that circumstances will unfold in a favorable manner. Direct your attention towards the various possibilities for success. In the event of unforeseen circumstances, make an effort to identify the silver lining in the given situation. By exerting sufficient effort in observation, it is possible to identify a positive aspect in any situation.

Find a Positive Distraction:

When you become aware of your mind veering towards that pessimistic realm of excessive rumination, engage in an activity that diverts your attention. Engage in literary pursuits, take a leisurely stroll, initiate a telephonic conversation with an acquaintance, engage in writing activities, proactively tackle pending tasks, and undertake any activity that aids in diverting your mind away from the ruminative thought process. Nevertheless, the undertaking you select ought to be constructive. Refrain from utilizing alcohol, drugs, or any other detrimental practices as a means to conceal or suppress one's thoughts. This can potentially give rise to highly detrimental practices and might only result in further harm.

Engage in cerebral introspection, albeit within defined temporal boundaries.

It can be mentally gratifying to dedicate a limited duration for contemplation on matters that tend to preoccupy the mind. If this brings about a sense of improvement in your well-being, allow your thoughts to stray or diverge for a duration of 5 to 10 minutes. Set a timer.

Upon the sounding of the timer, you are obliged to proceed to the next task. Gradually decrease the duration for which the timer is set as time progresses. You are deliberately conditioning your mind to refrain from fixating on distressing subjects. In due course, you will acquire the ability to swiftly relinquish your thoughts.

Recognize That Your Knowledge of Future Events is Limited: Acknowledge That You Are Unaware of What Lies Ahead: Comprehend That You Lack Certainty about Future Outcomes:

Your excessive contemplation may be focused on forthcoming occurrences. Irrespective of the extent of your preparations for the future, the unfolding of events remains beyond your control. Make necessary preparations for the aspects within your control and relinquish concerns over the elements beyond your influence. Be accepting of whatever the eventual result may be, with the understanding that you have the capability and resolve to persevere and overcome.

Strive for your utmost, and embrace it.

Frequently, the tendency to overthink arises from a sense of inadequacy or a lack of self-worth. This notion may have originated from prior occurrences where you perceived yourself to have fallen short, thereby giving rise to apprehension that history may veer towards a similar outcome. Approach every endeavor with unwavering dedication and commitment. Exhibiting your utmost capabilities is the only expectation you can have of yourself. In the event of an unfavorable outcome, it is commendable that you made the effort. It is unrealistic to anticipate achieving universal success as no individual excels in every aspect of life.

Compile an inventory of elements in your existence that instill a sense of gratitude within you.

Upon compiling this list, you may find yourself pleasantly astonished by the abundance of positive aspects that grace your life. It is readily possible for individuals to become excessively preoccupied with pessimistic aspects. This leads one to infer that their experiential background is inadequate. Observing the tangible manifestation of one's possessions can yield a profound impact. Please consult this list when you are feeling inundated or require a source of rejuvenation.

To liberate oneself from the habit of overthinking, it is essential to clear one's mind. Eliminate the negative aspects from your life and substitute them with positive ones. Excessive clutter and excessive rumination can give rise to significant mental health concerns. You possess the ability to assume authority over your cognitive processes and embark upon a course of efficiency and self-valorization.

The Authority bestowed upon one as a Representative of the Divine Entity

The role of a leader is to serve as an ambassador of the divine entity. During the ancient era, certain monarchs possessed the capacity to serve as intermediaries between the terrestrial world and the metaphysical realms. Consequently, individuals harbored profound adoration and respect for these leaders, perceiving them rightfully as divine emissaries in terrestrial form.

As a leader, it is incumbent upon you to cultivate a receptive mindset and embrace the potential of serving as a conduit for divine guidance, thereby embodying a spiritual conduit. One critical determinant of becoming a conduit of this nature is the quality of selflessness. When individuals under your supervision convey their loyalty, commitment, and assistance, it is incumbent upon you to acknowledge and utilize their contributions for the betterment of broader society, while perpetually transferring the benefits of these achievements to a higher power.

Put differently, a leader cannot lay any claim to being the executor or the manipulator. Through relinquishing these assertions and emotional dependencies, you surrender all your deeds and acquisitions to the Supreme Being, who will ultimately reciprocate by bestowing even greater abundance upon you. As an individual with a heightened awareness of spirituality, you occupy the intermediary position between the realm of the supernatural and our physical world. As one deepens their affection, they effectively enhance their capacity to serve as a conduit, facilitating the connection between those entrusted to their guidance and the elevated spheres. In this transitional role spanning the ethereal and tangible realms, you receive revelations and divine favor from higher planes and disseminate them to others, while also accepting assistance from those under your stewardship and redirecting the outcomes back to celestial spheres. By adopting this approach, you will elevate yourself as a person with authority and become a proficient leader.

Empowerment is everyone's right. By what means do certain individuals demonstrate extraordinary abilities, seemingly surpassing the limits of human capability, as if they are endowed with a unique divine favor? The uniqueness of the blessing lies not in its exclusivity, but rather in the willingness of these individuals to be receptive to it. Those individuals who fail to embrace the role of a benevolent servant, extending love and compassion to all, ultimately pose a significant obstacle. Hence, it is crucial to bear in mind that your actions are subject to scrutiny at a superior level whenever you engage in any activity. As the expansion of your compassion becomes more pronounced, your inclination towards rendering service will invariably intensify.

Willingness to Serve Others

Your eagerness to serve instills a sense of empowerment and significantly enhances the effectiveness of your service. The bestowal of empowerment from the divine realm occurs when you willingly contribute your skill set to aid others. Subsequently, these celestial and transcendent bonds shall reciprocate by bestowing upon you heightened obligations. This phenomenon is not out of the ordinary; a comparable procedure takes place among individuals employed in your workplace, involved in the administration of your government, or assisting you in the management of your corporation. As you observe individuals who demonstrate exceptional commitment by wholeheartedly delivering excellent service, you take measures to assign them more intricate and challenging responsibilities, thus promoting and rewarding them in acknowledgment of their unwavering dedication.

In a similar vein, by utilizing your resources judiciously and dedicating your leadership to the betterment of others, you will undoubtedly reap the rewards. Nevertheless, the inverse holds true as well. In the event that one fails to judiciously utilize the resources and authority bestowed upon them, it is inevitable that their subordinates will discern their lack of genuine concern for their welfare, culminating in their eventual downfall despite any transient apparent success they may experience.

It is crucial to comprehend this significant fact, as it is inevitable that certain of your plans may exhibit ineffectiveness or result in disappointment for others. The aforementioned errors become increasingly intolerable when individuals perceive that the leader lacks genuine concern for their welfare. Nevertheless, should individuals comprehend that their esteemed leader has been diligently endeavoring to assist them, such errors will not give rise to substantial adversities and might potentially enhance their allegiance.

One final admonition regarding the straightforward yet intricate nature of love: it is imperative to consistently endeavor to foresee in advance and evaluate afterwards the extent to which each of your strategies augments the affection of those under your guidance. Truly, a principal duty as a leader lies in demonstrating affection and facilitating the cultivation of love within others' lives. Failure to comprehend the fundamental aspects presented in this chapter may result in the forfeiture of your status, recognition, collaborative affiliations, sound physical condition, your mental well-being, or conceivably even your existence.

Cultivate a profound affection for all individuals and embrace the ability to emanate this compassionate love towards others. By allowing the powerful force of love to resonate within your being, those who harmonize with you will inevitably acquire this infectious, transcendent sensation, and fervently transmit it to others.

Highlights

Oftentimes, what individuals refer to as love can be identified as either sentimentalism or the aspiration for sensual gratification. This implies that for numerous individuals, what is commonly understood as love could in fact be attributed solely to egotism or carnal desires. In spite of the perpetual influence exerted on individuals by the conflicting forces of affection and self-indulgent desires, each person possesses the autonomy to make a conscious selection between them.

Actions that demonstrate a mature form of love are carried out with a sense of honesty and understanding. While it is true that truth can cause discomfort, leaders may occasionally need to confront unwelcome truths and express themselves assertively in order to achieve greater objectives and fulfill their responsibilities. Truly, affection only holds substance when it is founded on sincerity.

The inherent nature of the human race is characterized by spirituality and divinity, akin to that of God. However, humans possess finite capabilities, in contrast to the boundless power possessed by God. Stated differently, individuals possess a similar essence as God, yet differ in their measure or extent.

Any ideas, expressions, or behaviors that are aimed at the transcendental aspect of an individual will yield significantly more advantageous and enduring outcomes compared to those that are not.

One cannot extend love to others unless there is a substantial self-love, as it is implausible to bestow or distribute something that one does not possess. Frequently, assuming a leadership role poses challenges due to personality conflicts or due to strong affiliations with nationalism, racism, sexism, or tribalism. In order to effectively tackle such challenges, it is essential to cultivate a profound sense of love, which originates from recognizing the sacredness inherent within oneself.

In your capacity as a leader, perceive yourself as the custodian of those within your purview, instead of an owner, conducting yourself with the same care and diligence one would exercise when bestowed with a valuable commodity. This method promotes the acknowledgement of the divine essence within each individual, urging you to recognize yourself as a representative of the divine tasked with fostering the divine essence in others. Engaging in this manner of service towards God is among the utmost expressions of love attainable.

The role of a leader entails serving as a divine representative. As a leader, it is imperative for you to embrace the idea of being a divine emissary, thereby assuming a spiritual conduit, as part of your responsibilities. One crucial determinant in developing into such a conduit is the quality of selflessness.

As a leader who is deeply aware of spiritual matters, you occupy a position that bridges the gap between the realm of spirituality and the physical world. By augmenting your affection, you enhance your capacity as an instrument proficient in forging links between those under your guidance and the celestial domains. In this intermediary role that exists amidst the realms of the spiritual and material, you embrace and receive revelations and benevolence from elevated dimensions, subsequently disseminating them to others. Simultaneously, you accept the dutiful assistance of your constituents and redirect the outcomes back to the elevated realms. By adopting this approach, you will emerge as an empowered individual and a remarkably adept leader.

Cultivate a profound affection for all individuals and let this love emanate from within you. As the aura of love permeates your being, all those who associate themselves with you shall embrace this infectious, transcendent state, and fervently transmit it to others.

Persistently strive to anticipate in advance and evaluate afterward how each of your policies fosters a sense of affection among those whom you govern. Certainly, among the primary responsibilities bestowed upon you as a leader is to effectively convey affection and support others in cultivating their own sense of affection.

Mindsets

Please consult the initial section of this book, where you will find a list of ten indispensable technologies. Pay specific attention to numbers 7 and 8 as you proceed. Engage in the practice of embodying love in each of your interactions while regarding the actions of others as either manifestations of love or appeals for assistance.

Desire and affection are everlasting entities, two streams of vitality in perpetual motion within our surroundings. Envision yourself situated at the heart of an expansive body of water. If you opt to navigate towards the left, you shall find yourself being propelled by a compelling current of desire; on the contrary, by steering towards the right, you shall permeate an fervent current of affection. Make your choice. Recognize the resemblance between this and your everyday encounters, wherein you are constantly presented with the opportunity to select which course of action to pursue.

Even though love can be accompanied by pain in the face of honesty and awareness, it is important to reaffirm your commitment to unwavering integrity, even if others fail to comprehend your actions. This reminder aims to enhance your determination and fortify the positive ambiance surrounding you.

Envision situations where one finds themselves yielding to the desires of lust, noting that this is essentially a form of misguided affection. May these visuals serve as a potent deterrent, compelling you to refrain from engaging in similar conduct.

As a practice in cultivating self-love as a spiritual entity, engage in daily internal dialogue with your soul. Celebrate and acknowledge the essence of your being, and express gratitude towards yourself as a divine manifestation. Recognize that you are an integral element of the divine presence. Please bear in mind that one's ability to foster profound love for others is contingent upon their ability to cultivate a healthy sense of self-respect and self-worth.

You are a warrior. Envision yourself confronting detrimental energy by wielding the weapon of knowledge, wielding the shield of compassion, and donning the armor of love. This is particularly advantageous when engaging in negotiations with individuals of a divergent perspective, when facing opposition from adversaries, or when experiencing a sense of being misunderstood or undervalued in one's endeavors.

Continuously conduct a meticulous examination of your thoughts, words, and actions to ascertain if you demonstrate a love for your neighbor that is at least equal to, if not surpassing, the love you have for yourself. Be honest. If your thoughts are not in harmony, devote your attention to reconciling them with the force of love.

Perpetually perceive yourself as a custodian entrusted with the stewardship of God's possessions, handling everything under your guardianship with utmost reverence exceeding that which you would accord towards your personal belongings.

During antiquity, a leader held the dual status of being regarded as a divine emissary and a proficient steward, whose constructive endeavors engendered a deepened affection among the populace. Regard yourself as a leader of such caliber, and diligently engage in ongoing practice to uphold this state of awareness. As a representative of the divine, it is expected of you to graciously accept all that is presented to you, relinquishing any sense of personal ownership and faithfully offering everything unto the divine. Attribute your accomplishments to a higher power and demonstrate appreciation for your benevolence in bestowing your abundance upon those under your care.

Regard yourself as a conduit for an infectious love that permeates those around you as you traverse through life. Subsequently, those in your vicinity assume the role of emissaries, exemplifying an altruistic affection that extends to additional individuals.

Physical activity proves to be the most efficacious approach for coping with a difficult day.

A certain degree of stress is beneficial and essential for optimizing performance. At times, stress can indeed escalate. As a result, it is imperative that we effectively manage stress in order to prevent its escalation and the resultant burnout.

Numerous work-related situations can be characterized by high levels of stress, encompassing factors such as meeting strict deadlines, managing challenging personnel, maintaining a positive demeanor in customer interactions, receiving disciplinaries from superiors, encountering unsuccessful projects, engaging in corporate mergers, undergoing reorganizations, experiencing contract losses, witnessing decreased sales, and encountering unsuccessful product launches. When individuals are faced with stress, they encounter adverse emotional states. They develop a sense of discontentment regarding their employment, experience weariness, melancholy, and unease, and exhibit a diminished enthusiasm towards once-enjoyed pursuits and pastimes. Therefore, the following inquiry arises: What is the optimal approach to effectively mitigate these detrimental emotional states?

Over twenty years ago, psychologist Robert Thayer from California State University conducted a study in which individuals were requested to provide accounts of the most efficacious and prosperous methods they employed to navigate through a challenging day. Curiously, the majority of individuals cited physical activity as the foremost effective approach. Presented below are the findings of the survey, showcasing the ranking of tactics based on respondents' feedback, highlighting the most efficient strategies.

(1) Exercise

(2) Listening to music

(3) Engaging in telecommunications, conversing with, or accompanying an individual

(4) Tending to chores

(5) Engaging in a state of repose, reclining, or engaging in slumber

(6) Employing cognitive regulation techniques, such as managing thoughts, assessing or evaluating the situation, or gaining a balanced perspective on emotions.

(7) Implementing measures to steer clear of the source of the emotional state

(8) Being alone

The recent study conducted by Maxime Taquet at Harvard Medical School lends credence to the notion that exercise is the most efficacious approach in managing negative emotions. Taquet requested more than 28,000 individuals to divulge their immediate emotional state and current activities over a duration of roughly four weeks, utilizing a smartphone application that is accessible through various platforms. Taquet discovered a correlation between individuals experiencing negative emotions and their higher propensity for engaging in sporting activities. The aforementioned sports encompassed activities such as outdoor recreation, social interaction, cultural engagement, indulgence in refreshments, participation in games, and culinary experiences. Furthermore, engaging in sports elicited the most noteworthy improvement in mood in comparison to the alternative activities. Here is the presented listing of the most successful approaches employed by individuals:

(1) Sport

(2) Nature

(3) Culture

(4) Leisure

(5) Chatting

(6) Drinking

(7) Playing

(8) Eating

Engaging in physical activity is the most efficacious approach to cope with a challenging day.

A second inquiry that arises is: To what extent does physical activity need to be undertaken in order to bolster one's emotional well-being and alleviate stress? Robert Thayer conducted a study which revealed that a mere ten-minute session of brisk walking has the ability to alleviate feelings of tension and diminish the perceived severity of diverse personal issues. Furthermore, it should be noted that this holds ample capacity to enhance both vitality and positive outlook. The duration of certain effects may persist for up to a maximum of two hours subsequent to engaging in a walking activity.

During periods of heightened stress, numerous individuals resort to consuming sugary snacks as a form of comfort food, engaging in smoking, or resorting to alcohol consumption as a means of coping. These coping mechanisms have the capacity to alter individuals' perception of stress and difficulties, thereby diminishing negative emotions, albeit only temporarily. Nevertheless, over time, they prove to be deleterious to both the physical and mental wellbeing, thereby diminishing individuals' capacity for problem-solving. According to an ancient proverb from China, there exists a phrase known as yinzhenzhike, which metaphorically suggests satisfying one's thirst with a substance that is poisonous. Engaging in the consumption of unhealthy foods, engaging in smoking, and resorting to alcohol as a means of stress relief serve as common illustrations of yinzhenzhike.

According to Thayer's research, engaging in a brisk ten-minute walk is found to be more efficacious in enhancing energy levels and reducing tension compared to consuming a candy bar. Additionally, engaging in a brief five-minute walk prior to consuming a cigarette or indulging in a sugary treat substantially diminishes the desire to smoke or indulge while prolonging the interval until engaging in the next cigarette or snack consumption. It implies that engaging in physical activity may serve as a viable alternative to smoking or snacking in order to elevate mood and alleviate stress. In addition to walking, engaging in any form of physical exercise or athletic activity has proven to be advantageous in bolstering an individual's emotional state. Numerous studies have provided compelling evidence that a solitary bout of physical activity, encompassing various forms such as cycling, running, jogging, swimming, dancing, or yoga, is connected to a decline in perceived levels of stress, fatigue, anxiety, depression, and an enhancement of energy and vitality. These observations offer compelling evidence that endorses exercise as an effective strategy for mitigating stress and managing mood.

In the event that you experience a day filled with negativity, consider engaging in physical activity as a means to rejuvenate and replenish your energy. When you find it necessary to engage in discussions regarding issues with your employees or superiors, kindly suggest going for a stroll or engaging in a physical activity together. You have the option to address the issue either during or post your physical activity session. It alleviates the tension and perceived stress experienced by both your subordinates and superiors, in addition to yourself. A win-win situation.

Strengthening Your Team

Upon the enlistment of new members onto your team, your primary responsibility is to provide them with training. Irrespective of their level of expertise in your industry, individuals are still required to familiarize themselves with the nuances of collaborating with your organization and its personnel.

Essential leaders ensure the seamless assimilation of a new team member by leveraging the managerial and visionary abilities, thus guaranteeing a positive onboarding process for the newly recruited individual. Indeed, it is imperative to verify the implementation of the necessary technical training. Furthermore, it is imperative to provide ample opportunity for the incoming individual to foster connections and integrate seamlessly into the team, organization, and corporate environment. Right from the beginning, it is crucial to promptly initiate the establishment of rapport and credibility. I cannot emphasize this aspect strongly enough: credibility forms the bedrock upon which one establishes a self-sufficient, reliable, and devoted team.

In order to attain optimal performance, it is imperative that all team members, including the leader, possess complete reliance in one another. In the absence of reciprocal trust, a team will find itself ensnared in a recurring state of uncertainty, dissatisfaction, and unease. Consequently, this outcome will impede the team's ability to innovate and generate ideas, which are crucial elements for effectively expanding a business or department.

In order to ascertain credibility, exceedingly proficient Indispensable Leaders cultivate a enduring association of reverence with both their team members and among them. The practice entails consistently ensuring that your team's voices are heard - not solely through implementing an open-door policy, but through actively seeking to comprehend your team's perspectives. Active participation and inquiry are encouraged. Display a genuine inquisitiveness towards your team members, encompassing both their professional and personal lives. Engaging in such behavior does not necessitate the obligation to establish a friendly relationship and partake in social activities outside of work. The concept entails demonstrating genuine concern for their professional growth, personal life, and accomplishments, ensuring that they are aware of your profound interest. This high measure of engagement will effectively foster genuine credibility and foster an elevation of trust, thereby positioning you for future success. A team that places their trust in and holds their leader in high regard is willing to surpass expectations and excel under their guidance.

Undoubtedly, there is a period for deliberation and a period to transition into implementation. Bruce expressed the belief that collaborative effort yields superior results, regardless of hierarchical reporting structures or equal positions amongst individuals. I firmly adhered to gathering input from a wide range of sources in order to make an informed and well-considered decision. However, after the conclusion of that decision-making process, the ultimate responsibility fell upon me. I remained dedicated to it until the end."

When deemed necessary, a Leader of Utmost Importance possesses the discernment to conclude the phase of acquiring information and imparts challenging judgments to eliminate any form of ambiguity. It is imperative that you articulate your decisions in a compassionate and considerate manner, and make continual efforts to treat all individuals equitably.

A leader of great importance also comprehends that fairness does not always equate to equality. Attainment of equality might not be feasible in every instance. To illustrate, when team members perceive that equitable compensation is awarded to individuals who exhibit lower performance levels, it is often observed that teams experience adverse effects. The discrepancy has the potential to undermine both motivation and trust. Hence, instead of striving for equality, the Indispensable Leader endeavors to establish fairness.

A Fresh Perspective

It is important to remain vigilant of stagnant perspectives seeping into the imperative of resolving issues. Bonnie expressed, "I have come to understand the importance of seeking the perspective of an impartial third party to assess a situation when encountering challenges." Bonnie proceeded to provide a couple of illustrative instances. She was aware that she had to terminate the employment of a young sailor in a department under her authority. However, prior to dismissing him, she notes that she had interviewed another individual who assessed the situation and gathered statements from the coworkers. I subsequently enlisted the presence of an additional individual to assess the situation. I possessed a collection of documented statements and concerns, outlining certain actions carried out by the aforementioned young sailor. The investigators acknowledged that my actions went beyond relying solely on hearsay as I had conducted a preliminary inquiry into the concerns raised within his department."

However, according to Bonnie's guidance, it is important to not limit the invitation of a new perspective solely to situations involving problems. A third-party intervention can also prove advantageous in facilitating the expression of any potentially suppressed, valuable insights or ideas within your team. I would suggest the inclusion of a facilitator," she remarks, "as it has been observed that there exists a wealth of brilliant ideas among individuals, albeit their reluctance to consistently express them. In order to disseminate significant concepts, an intermediary is occasionally necessary. I am uncertain whether it is due to their fear or simply their hesitation to raise these matters. However, there are numerous individuals who possess valuable insights and innovative concepts, provided that they are given the necessary encouragement to express their thoughts."

Always Be Coaching

Commencement of the coaching process at the early stages of a new employee's tenure is imperative. Essential leaders allocate a substantial amount of time towards providing guidance and mentoring to their teams, both collectively and individually. The attention serves several functions: enhancing open communication, fostering trust and credibility, providing opportunities for sharing feedback and establishing explicit expectations, uncovering the hidden skills and talents of team members, and cultivating an inclusive environment where all voices are valued.

As stated by Jennifer Robinson in her 2020 Gallup article, "Astute managers understand that exceptional performance is cultivated through regular, substantive dialogues with their employees." They do not tolerate "remote control management." They possess comprehensive knowledge of their employees, enabling meaningful discussions that enhance performance and cultivate authentic relationships."

As a Vital Leader, it is imperative to exemplify commendable actions and behaviors that convey the message to your team that "If I am unwilling to undertake a task, how can I expect someone else to do so?" This principle is one that I ardently stand by, drawing from my personal experience, as it effectively mitigates employee attrition.

I made reference to the issue of employee turnover in a prior section. High employee attrition remains a significant concern within certain industries, and, in my view, it is evident that this issue primarily stems from deficiencies in leadership pertaining to recruitment, training, and coaching methods. Nevertheless, during my tenure as a manager at the 22-screen megaplex movie theater, I was assigned the responsibility of reducing the theater's employee attrition rate. At the onset, there was a significant turnover in personnel. The rate of turnover among the theater staff, consisting of over 100 individuals, essentially amounted to three times per year.

I undertook several initiatives to achieve that ambitious objective. Foremost among these tasks was fostering a sense of trust and reverence among the staff, a task rendered even more formidable by the circumstance that, in numerous instances, I shared a similar age range with those under my guidance. In order to foster trust and garner respect from my staff, I made a pledge to refrain from requesting tasks that I myself would not undertake. I exerted substantial effort in exemplifying the desired actions and behaviors to be emulated by them.

On a certain occasion, I received a communication through the radio requesting assistance in tending to the maintenance needs of the men's restroom. There had been an instance of regurgitation on the floor by an individual. Evidently, the assignment was not one that I anticipated with enthusiasm. However, acknowledging the potential of the situation, I expeditiously communicated via radio to inform the team that I would attend to the matter. It was a dreadful experience, but it also held substantial value. Subsequently, in the evening, another manager came up to me and inquired, "Why did you not simply request assistance from one of the team members to rectify the situation?" That is within their responsibilities." I explained, "I am striving to establish a cohesive team that values mutual respect, and I viewed this as an occasion to demonstrate my willingness to fulfill the tasks that I expect from them.

From that day forward, I saw a marked change in how the staff interacted with me. The action I took achieved precisely the intended objective I had envisioned.

Certain circumstances can be more amenable to alteration than others. For instance, assuming a fresh leadership role, particularly from an external standpoint, presents certain benefits as it allows for an unbiased viewpoint untainted by the current framework. However, if one is not cautious, it can have adverse effects as well.

An integral facet of team dynamics lies in the manner in which team members engage with each other, a responsibility that falls upon you, their esteemed leader. It is crucial for team members to experience not only being listened to, but also being comprehended, as this fosters a sense of worth. As you witness your team engaging in practices that you perceive to be incorrect or suboptimal in terms of efficiency, it is imperative to acknowledge the potential existence of underlying justifications for their methods and approaches. This observation presents a valuable chance to provide guidance and mentorship to your team members. Instead of impulsively expressing feedback or criticism, it is imperative for you, in your capacity as an Essential Leader, to endeavor to comprehend the rationale and motivations behind your team's actions. Were they trained wrong? Was erroneous information provided to them? Alternatively, they may possess insights that are outside your knowledge. Obtaining their input enables you to acquire insights into the underlying reasons behind their actions. Additionally, it provides you with the chance to utilize that information to serve as a mentor, aiding them in enhancing their skills and advancing their performance in their designated position.

Engaging in the mentorship of team members should not be limited solely to performance evaluations. Indeed, it is the utmost inappropriate setting for coaching to take place. A leader of utmost importance holds routine meetings and conducts individual interactions with their team members. These interactions afford you the chance to acquire a deeper understanding of their circumstances, encompassing not only the obstacles they face but also their aspirations and any apprehensions they may harbor regarding the team, the company, or their position.

Employing the process of coaching consistently and engaging in discussions pertaining to acquired knowledge mitigates the risk of losing team members due to unforeseen issues. If you limit your discussions solely to annual reviews, there is a strong possibility that you may miss out on valuable insights regarding the factors that may have caused frustration or discontent among team members, potentially resulting in the loss of a valuable member. While occasional deviations may occur, they ought to be infrequent. Invariably, astute leaders are rarely caught off guard by the departures of team members.

Recognition

Acknowledging your employees is an imperative undertaking if you aspire to foster genuine camaraderie among your team constituents. In my personal opinion, I would recommend that you make an effort to familiarize yourself with the names of their spouse and children. I have also come across suggestions stating that it would be advantageous to acquaint oneself with the names of their pets, though I personally have never gone to such lengths. Authentic leadership commences with taking the initiative to familiarize oneself with each member comprising the team. Ensure that, on the inaugural day of their employment, you acquaint the individual with the entire team and express your gratitude for their presence, conveying your anticipation for the forthcoming collaboration. In the event that an employee expresses their intention to resign in advance, it is advisable to procure a parting card for them and afford the opportunity for fellow colleagues to append their signatures. This gesture conveys your appreciation for the individuals who remain with the team, highlighting their importance as valuable team members. Furthermore, it assures them that you will show them due respect if they eventually decide to pursue different opportunities. If you seek inspiration regarding acknowledgment, The Carrot Principle penned by Adrian Gostick and Chester Elton would serve as an excellent resource. Outlined below are a few of the concepts that resonated with me as I read through the book:

1. A valuable takeaway can be derived from the practices of the boy scouts, advocating the necessity of preparedness. Ensure that gift cards are readily available for rewarding workers who consistently demonstrate exceptional performance or adhere to safety protocols.

2. Ensure that you address individuals by their respective names whenever you engage in conversation with them.

3. Commendation ought to be expressed openly, whereas censure deserves to be conveyed discreetly.

www.ingramcontent.com/pod-product-compliance
Lightning Source LLC
Chambersburg PA
CBHW050247120526
44590CB00016B/2244